THE GRAFFITI DOODLE BOOK

THE GRAFFITI DOODLE BOOK

Andrew Pinder

A PERIGEE BOOK

A PERIGEE BOOK
Published by the Penguin Group
Penguin Group (USA) Inc.
375 Hudson Street, New York, New York 10014, USA
Penguin Group (Canada), 90 Eglinton Avenue East, Suite 700, Toronto, Ontario M4P 2Y3, Canada
(a division of Pearson Penguin Canada Inc.)
Penguin Books Ltd., 80 Strand, London WC2R 0RL, England
Penguin Group Ireland, 25 St. Stephen's Green, Dublin 2, Ireland (a division of Penguin Books Ltd.)
Penguin Group (Australia), 250 Camberwell Road, Camberwell, Victoria 3124, Australia
(a division of Pearson Australia Group Pty. Ltd.)
Penguin Books India Pvt. Ltd., 11 Community Centre, Panchsheel Park, New Delhi—110 017, India
Penguin Group (NZ), 67 Apollo Drive, Rosedale, Auckland 0632, New Zealand
(a division of Pearson New Zealand Ltd.)
Penguin Books (South Africa) (Pty.) Ltd., 24 Sturdee Avenue, Rosebank, Johannesburg 2196,
South Africa

Penguin Books Ltd., Registered Offices: 80 Strand, London WC2R 0RL, England

While the author has made every effort to provide accurate telephone numbers and
Internet addresses at the time of publication, neither the publisher nor the author assumes
any responsibility for errors or for changes that occur after publication. Further, the publisher
does not have any control over and does not assume any responsibility for author or
third-party websites or their content.

THE GRAFFITI DOODLE BOOK

First American edition: February 2012
Originally published in Great Britain in 2011 as Graffiti Doodle by Michael O'Mara Books Limited.

ISBN: 978-0-399-53731-8

PRINTED IN THE UNITED STATES OF AMERICA

10 9 8 7 6 5 4 3 2 1

Most Perigee books are available at special quantity discounts for bulk purchases for sales
promotions, premiums, fund-raising, or educational use. Special books, or book excerpts, can also
be created to fit specific needs. For details, write: Special Markets, Penguin Group (USA) Inc.,
375 Hudson Street, New York, New York 10014.

Stonehenge

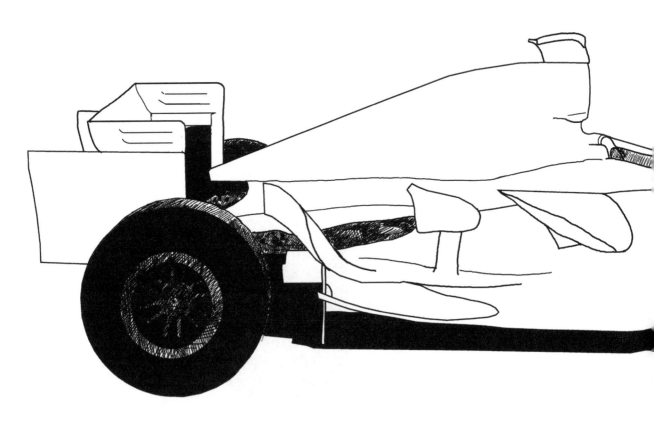

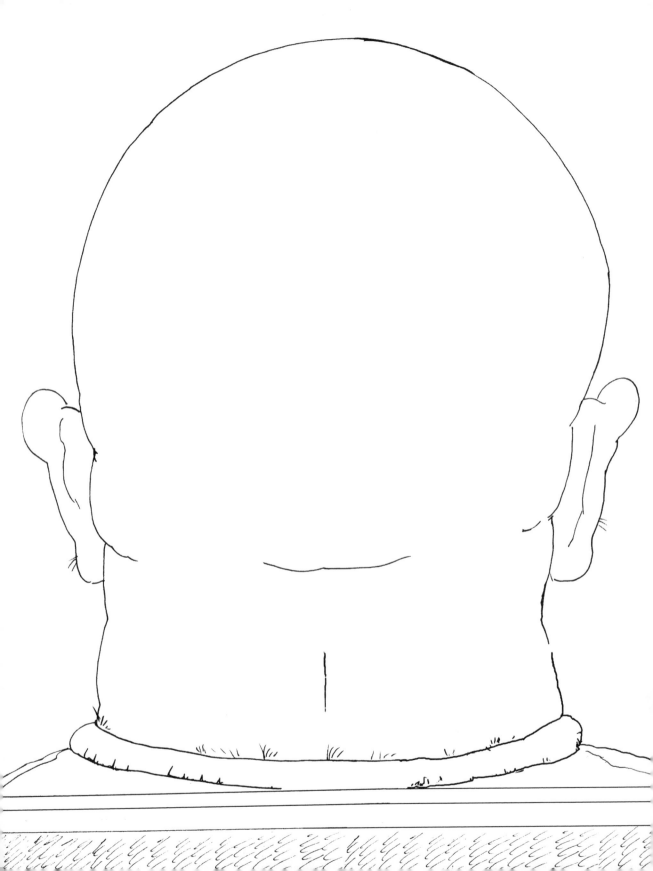

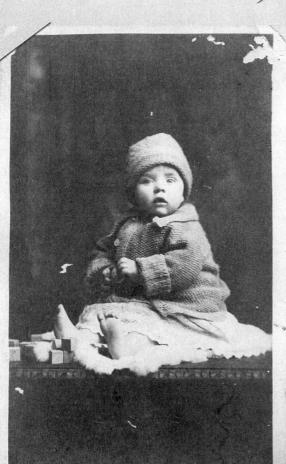

The Family Album

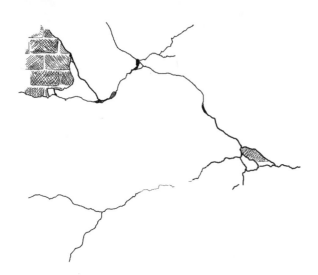

POST NO BILLS

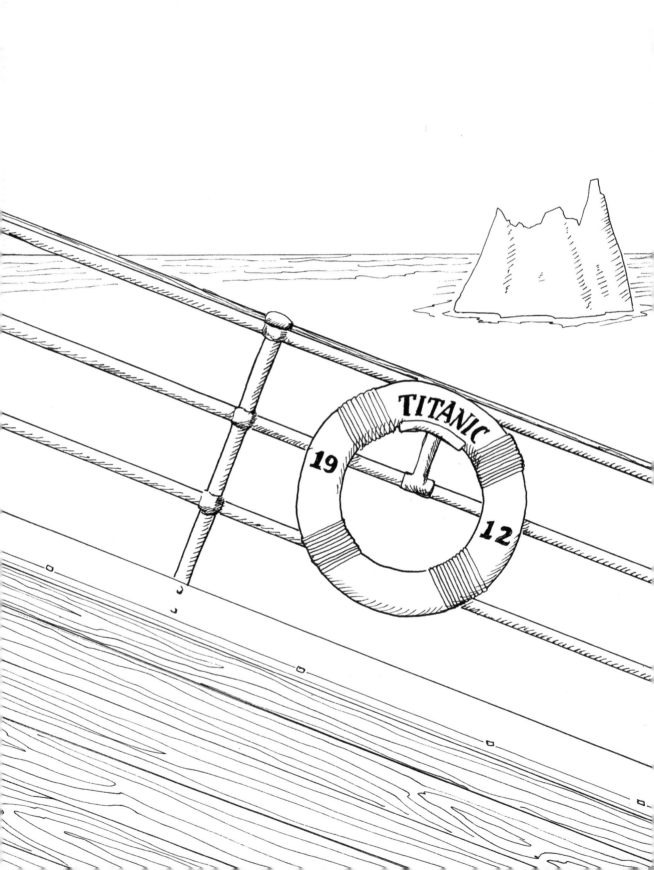

Château de Villandry, France

Casablanca (1942)

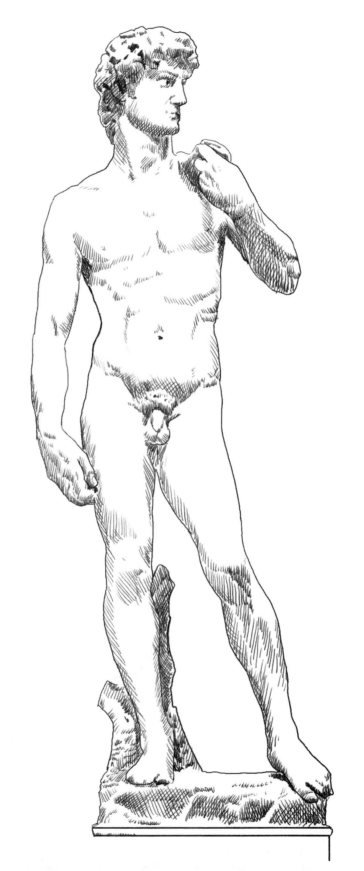

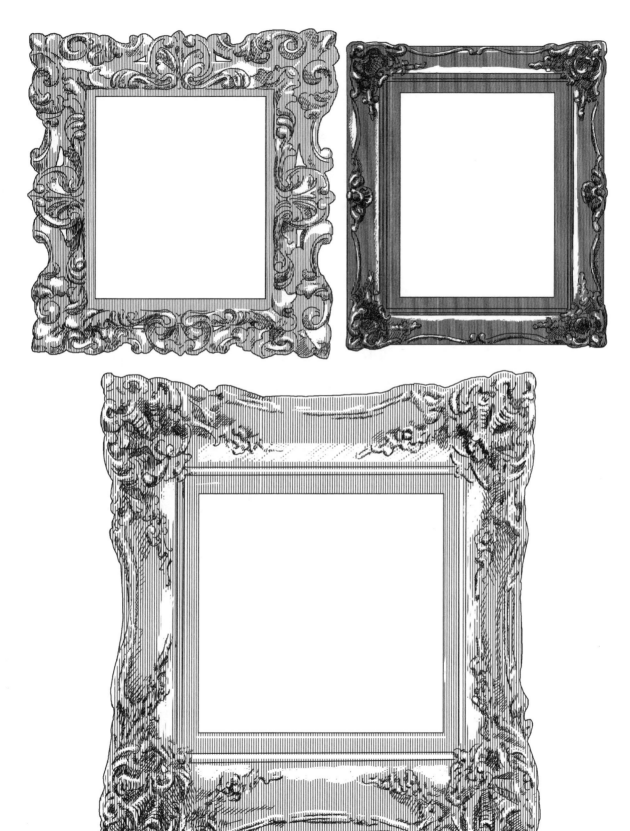

The Grand Canyon

Paradise Lost, Gustave Doré (c. 1866)

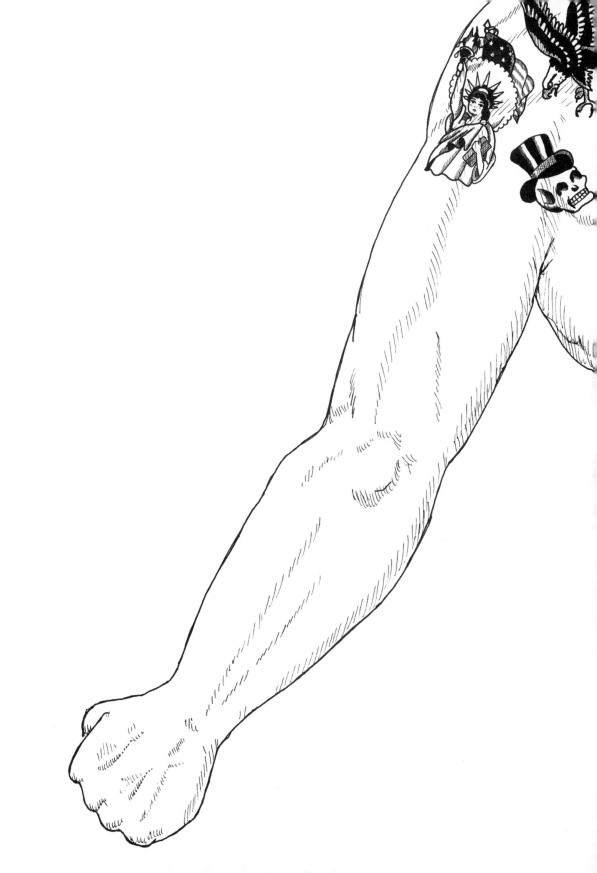

The Great Wave Off Kanagawa, Hokusai (c. 1830)

Tutankhamen

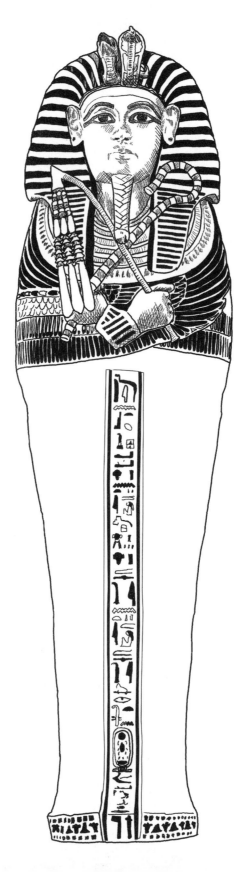

Buckingham Palace

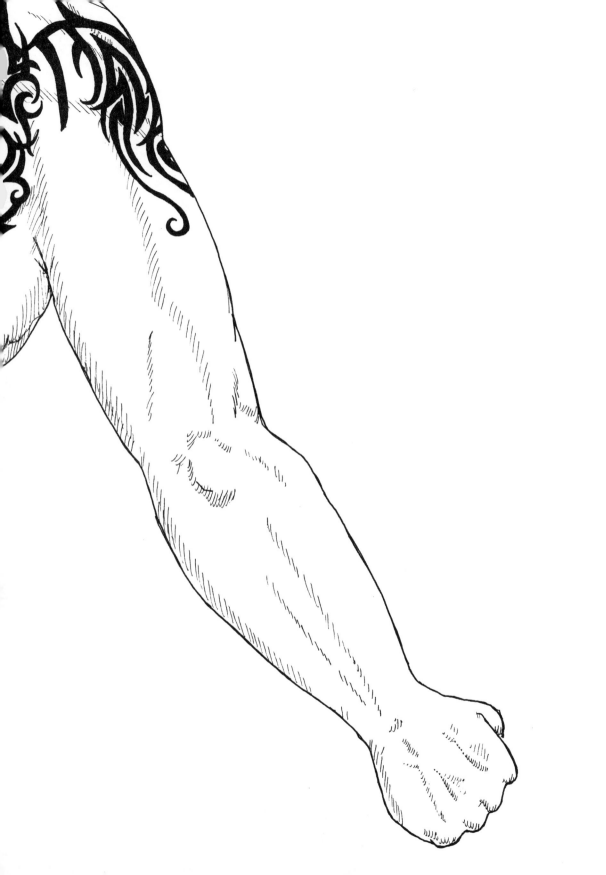

Jumbo the elephant,
Barnum & Bailey Circus (1882)

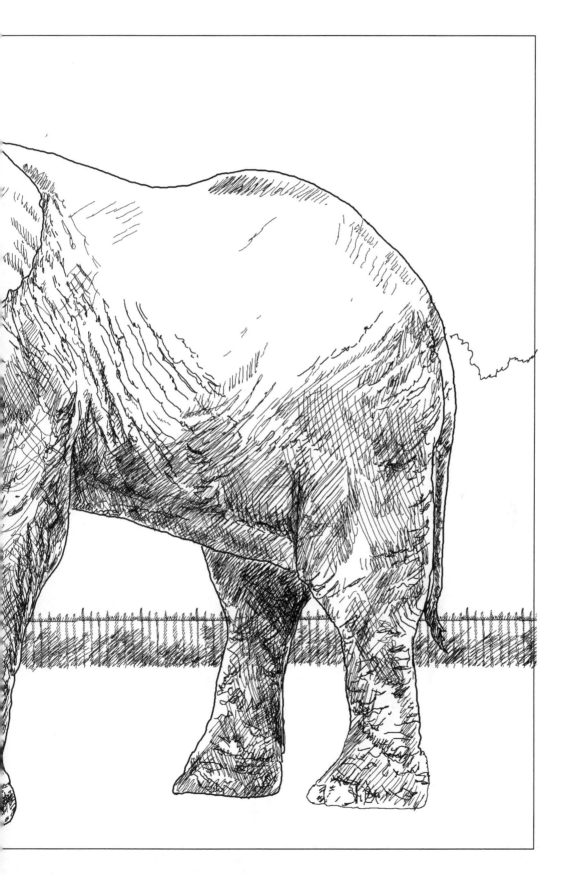

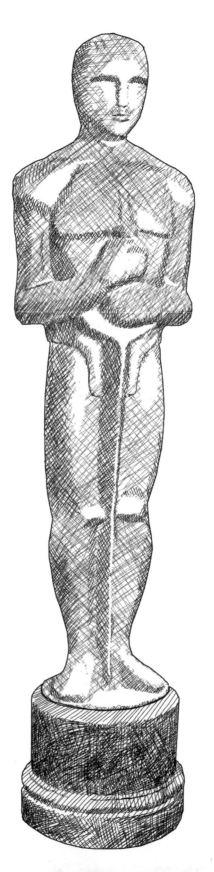

HASTA LA VICTORIA SIEMPRE

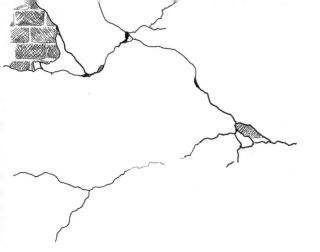

POST NO BILLS

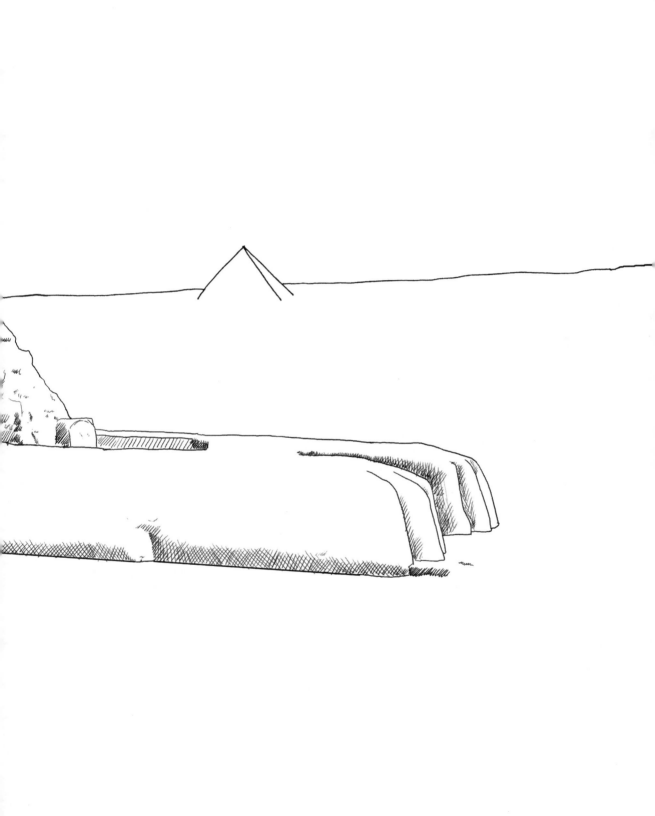

"Danse Macabre," *Nuremberg Chronicle* (1493)

The Three Graces, Peter Paul Rubens (c. 1636)

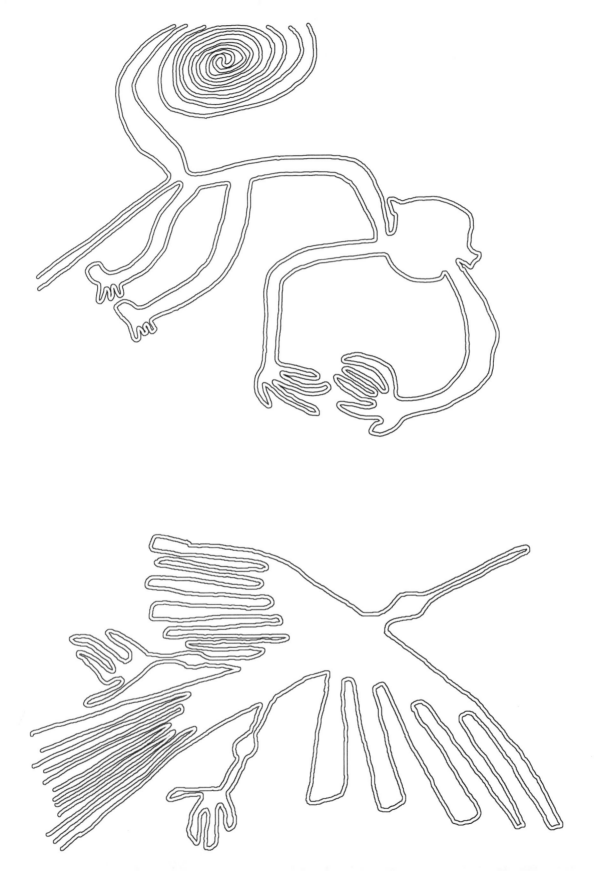

Nazca Lines, Peru (c. AD 500)

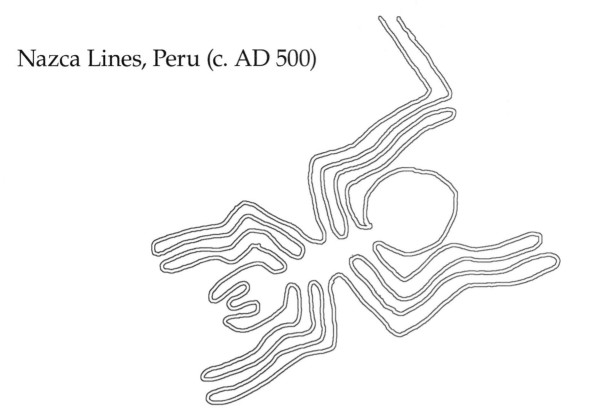

Hoover Dam

Arrangement in Grey and Black, James McNeill Whistler (1871)

Lascaux, France

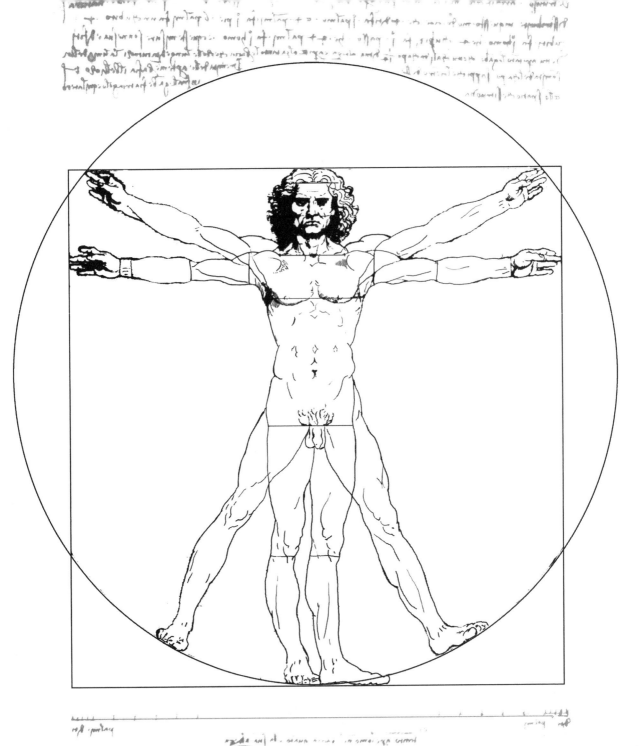

The Great Wall of China

Opera House, Sydney

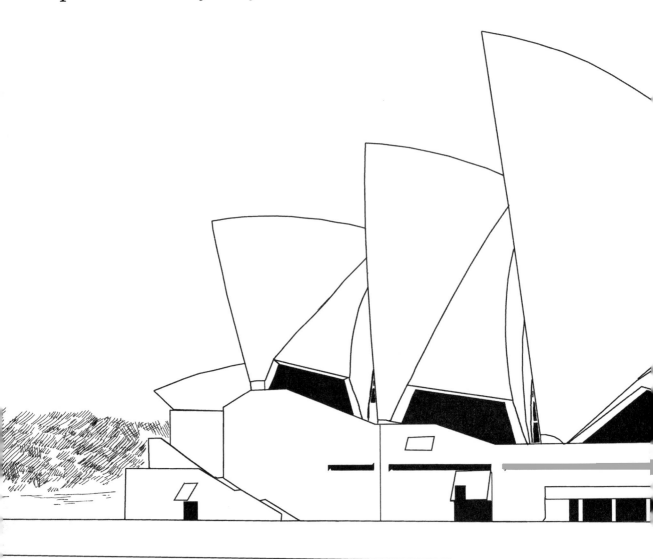

Superman #1 (1939)

Fort Knox

Tomb of Karl Marx, Highgate Cemetery, London

FV 4201 Chieftain tank (1960–70s)

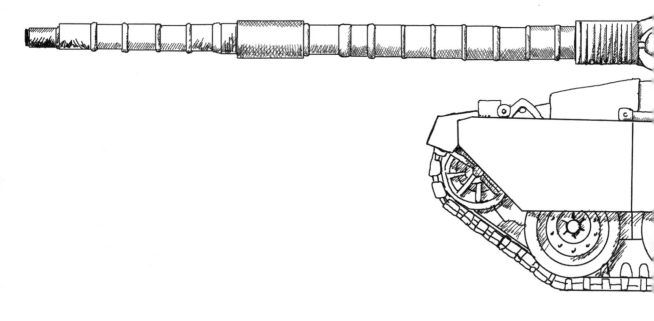

Papyrus of Ani (c. 1240 BC)

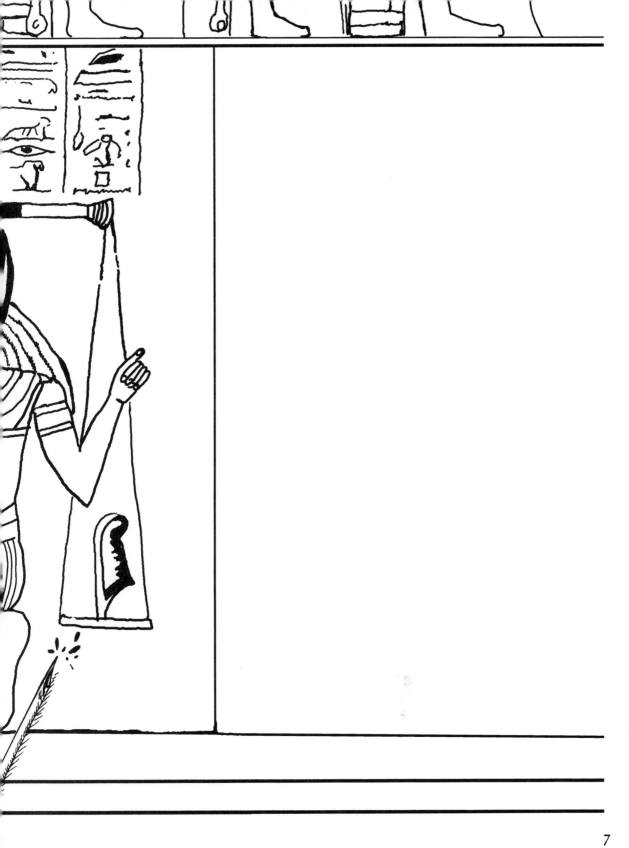

Barranco de la Valltorta, Spain

LVDC. DAVID
1812

OPVS

Tarzan

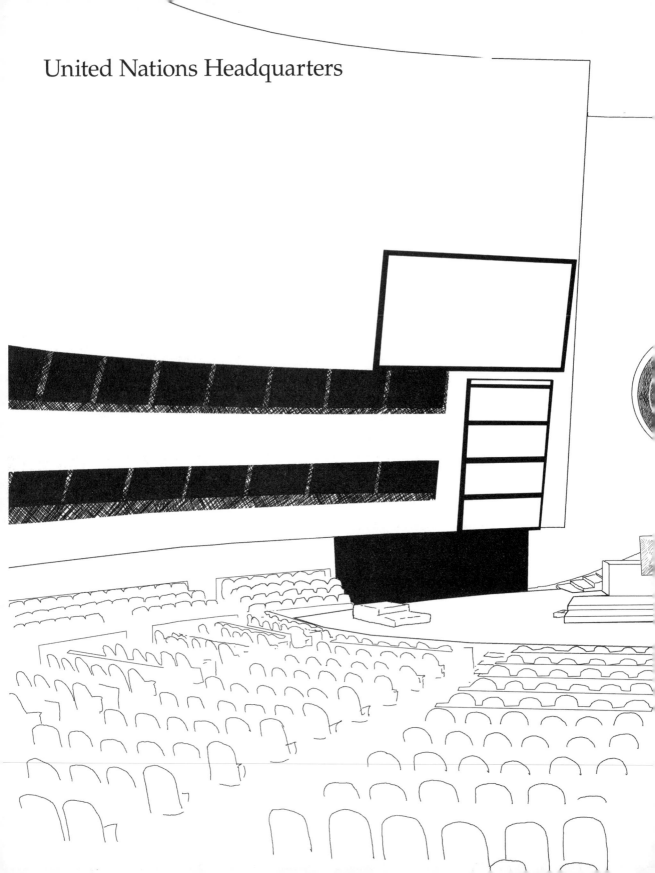

United Nations Headquarters

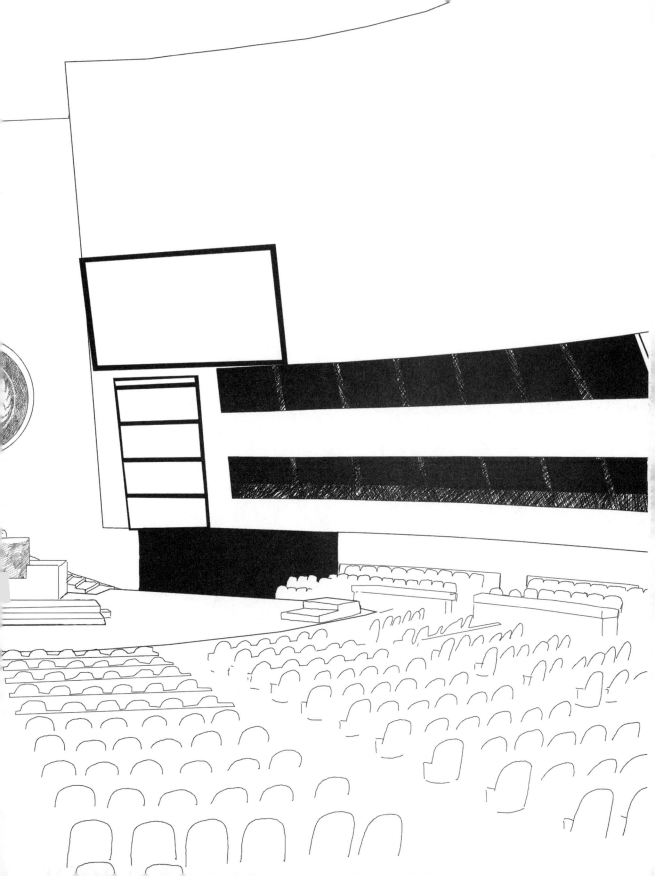

Gone With the Wind (1939)

The hills are alive . . .

10 Downing Street, London

The Beatles, Abbey Road

Cadillac (1959)

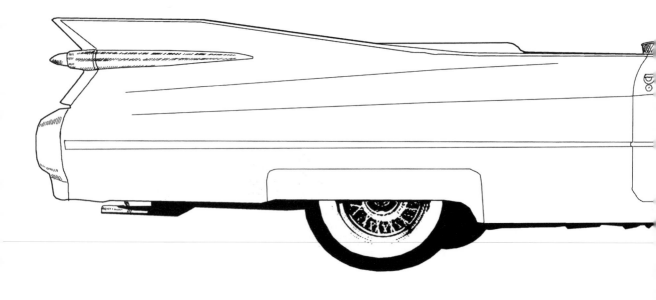

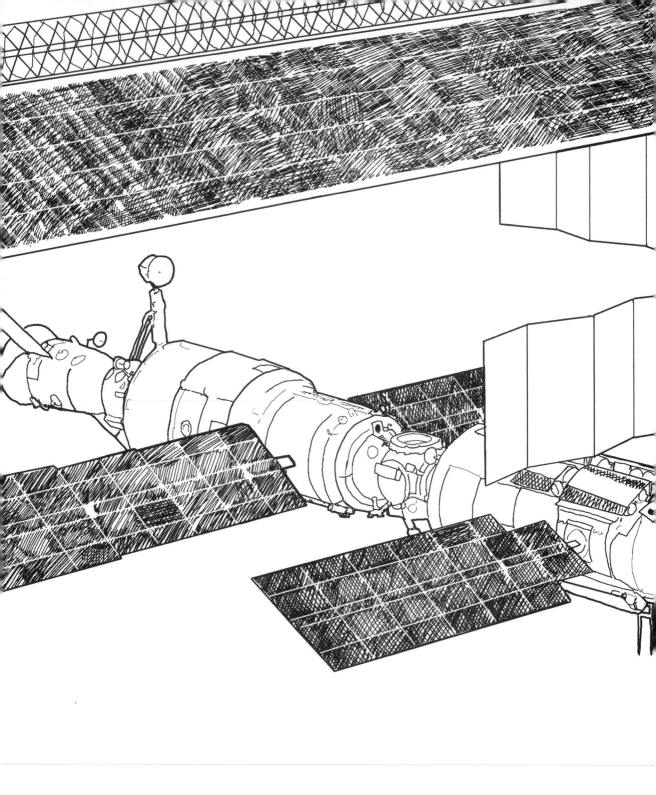

International Space Station

St. Basil's Cathedral, Red Square, Moscow

Bedroom in Arles,
Vincent van Gogh (1888)

Doge's Palace, Venice

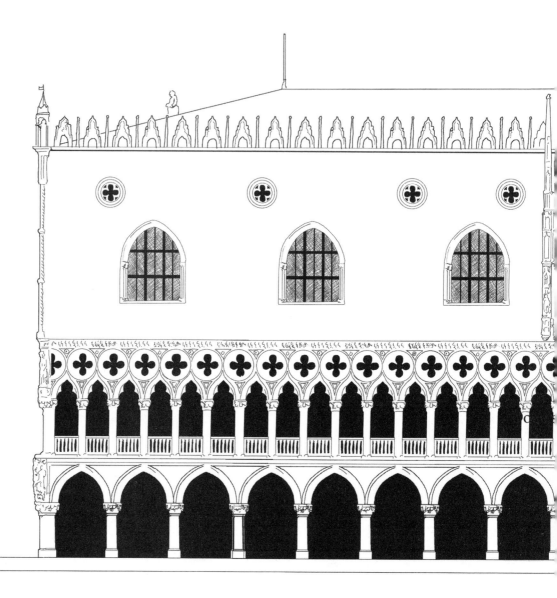

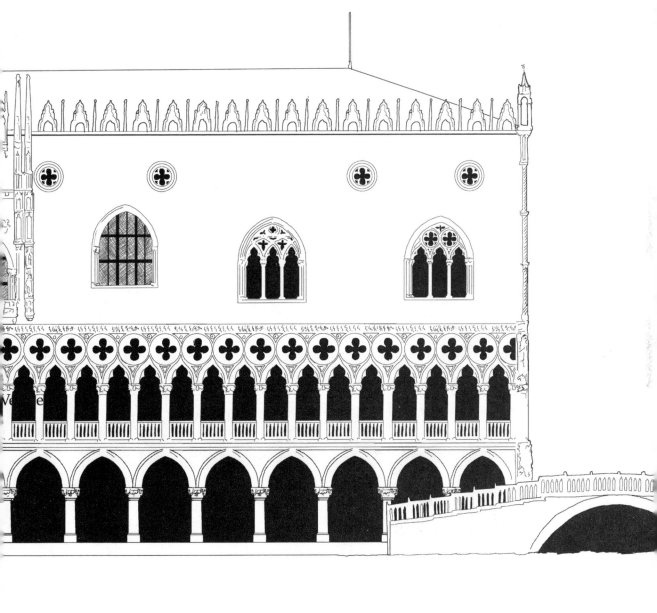

Washington Crossing the Delaware,
Emanuel Gottlieb Leutze (1851)

The White House

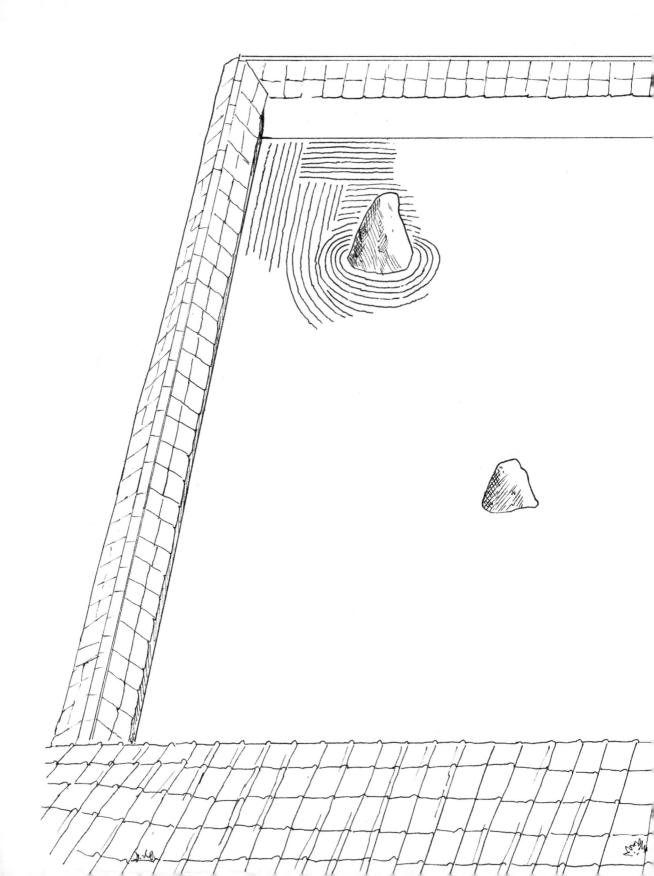

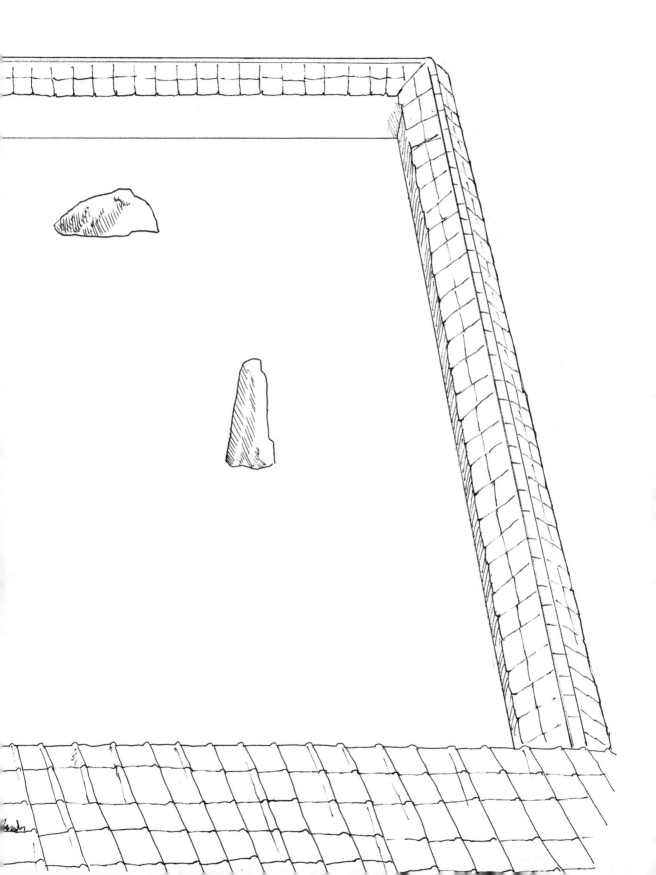

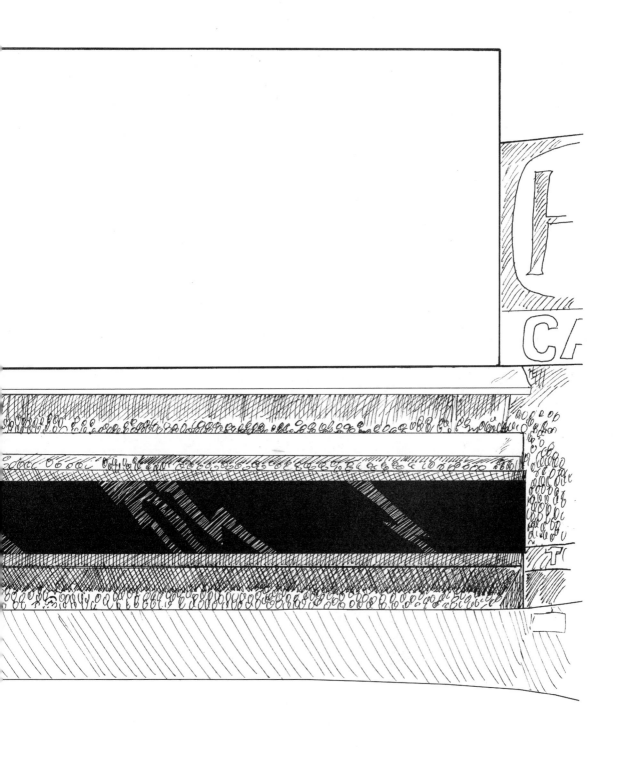